Story and lyrics by Jane E. Dickerson
Illustrations and music by Janice Rhoads Stetina
Guitar notes by Jo Manship-Loo

Printed on acid-free paper

This book and others listed at
www.LaurelwithaMoral.com
Orders fulfilled: www.Music44.com
Toll free: 1-866-419-6497

DICKERSON & RHOADS PRODUCTIONS
To contact author: 1-317-501-0742

RHOADS-STETINA GRAPHICS
Printed in the United States of America.
Library of Congress Control Number: applied for
ISBN: 978-0-9820628-0-7

LAUREL

with a
MORAL
PRESENTS

Do you really want to be
THE
QUEEN
OF
TURKEYS ?

Jane E. Dickerson, M.S.
author and educator

Janice Rhoads Stetina, Ph.D.
illustrator

This book belongs to ＿＿＿＿＿＿＿ .

The cackling and the giggling from the hen house came

As all the lady turkeys talked and hoped of coming fame.

A contest was a'comin' to a neighboring "barnyardy"——

to be the **"Queen of Turkeys"**——
what a *gala kind of party* !

To announce this beauty pageant
many posters had been sent.

Hens found advice for looking nice
as on and on they went——

Planning how to hold their wings
and how to strut with style,

Fluffing feathers and practicing
took quite a little while.

Others in the barnyard
        watched with due concern

They expressed their fears —

But from those mirrors,
turkey faces *would not turn.*

A horse with *stable* thinking said,

"When they announce the winner,
they may call that turkey 'beautiful,'
but they'll think —

Thanksgiving dinner !"

The turkeys wouldn't listen to him,
      nor heed the rabbit's warning sounds.

They said, "Rabbit, you're just tired and old,
      and that makes you *out of bounds.*"

THUMP!
THUMP!
THUMP!

They ignored the frogs and polliwogs,
who croaked warnings loud and low.

"It won't be fun when you are *done*
to say we *'toad'* ya' so !"

The barnyard boys had one last plan

to warn them of their doom.

They'd not snooze, 'til their kazoos

could hum a warning tune.

Soon everything was ready
and the judges took their stand.

The barnyard boys made more than noise
      when they struck up the band.

They sang:
    Step back and take a long-long look
    when your looks are looked at long.

    It's who you are —
        not how you look—
or watch out 'cause something's wrong !

Verse:

Flattery's a thin disguise. It really can confuse you.
It sounds so nice, but you'd better think twice.
It may be used to *use you*.

Chorus:

So, step back and take a long, long look
when your looks are looked at long.
It's who you are — not how you look —
or watch out 'cause something's wrong !

Everyone enjoyed the music.   It had a barnyard beat.

But the words got in the head of one —
and not just in her feet.

That turkey took a *long-long look*
and much to her surprise,

One judge, *he looked familiar* ———

She grabbed her friend

and home they ran

just in the nick of time.

Now, you'll hear them tell this tale
with this catchy little rhyme:

Chorus:
Step back and take a long-long look
when your looks are looked at long.

It's who you are——not how you look——
        or watch out
          'cause something's wrong !

Verse:
Don't get used, you'll feel abused.

Consider the thoughts behind it.

The words have force,
        so, study the source.

If it's flattery, you'll find it.

LONG-LONG LOOK

Lyrics by Jane Dickerson
Music by J. Rhoads Stetina

Guitar Notes by Troy Stetina

Step back ! Take a long-long look when your looks are looked at long. It's

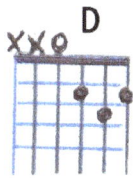
D

Em

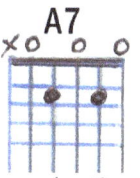
A7

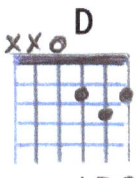
D

1. Flat---ter---y's a thin dis---guise. It real--ly can con----fuse you. it
2. Don't get used, you'll feel a---bused. Con---sider the thoughts be--hind it. The

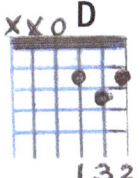
D

Em

sounds so nice, but you'd bet----ter think twice. It
words have force, so stud----y the source. If it's

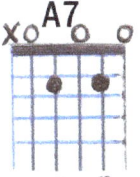
A7

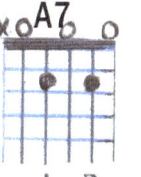
A7

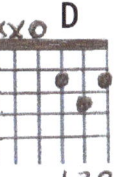
D

D.C.al Fine

may be used to use you. So
flat-------ter----------y, you'll find it. So

JANE E. DICKERSON, M.S.
author and educator

LAUREL

with a
MORAL

Teacher for 16 years
Positions: Pre-school (Special Ed)
        Kindergarten
        5th, 6th, 7th grades
        Winter-term college course
        Substitute teaching provided experience
                in all other grade levels.

Children's Television Writer/Producer
"The Filling Station"
a character-building program
for kids from 1 to 100

Winner of *10 national awards for TV*
8 Angel Awards
1 National Religious Broadcasters' Award
1 A.C.E. Award (highest honor in Cable TV)

Business Woman
Owner of **3D Productions**
Writing and producing commercials,
infomercials, and corporate videos

Children's Author
Stories, songs, plays, skits, including
her series *"Laurel with a Moral"*

Curriculum Developer
"Hands of Champions"
a supplemental math program

MORE STORIES THAT INSPIRE ME:

_____

_____

_____

_____

_____

_____

_____

_____

_____

_____

Collect all in the series

LAUREL WITH A MORAL

www.ingramcontent.com/pod-product-compliance
Lightning Source LLC
Chambersburg PA
CBHW041224040426
42443CB00002B/78